365
Provocative
Questions for
Young Women
Aged 18-19

365 Provocative Questions for Young Women Aged 18-19

One Question a Day to Forge Independence and Shape Their Future

Aria Capri Publishing
Devon Abbruzzese
Mauricio Vasquez

Toronto, Canada

365 Provocative Questions for Young Women Aged 18-19 by Aria Capri Publishing [Aria Capri International Inc.]. All Rights Reserved.

Authors:
Devon Abbruzzese
Mauricio Vasquez
Aria Capri Publishing

First Printing: May 2024

ISBN-978-1-998402-52-6 (Paperback book)
ISBN-978-1-998402-51-9 (Hardcover book)
ISBN-978-1-998402-50-2 (Electronic book)

Introduction

Welcome to a journey beyond the surface of adolescent development, delving into the profound impact of thoughtful questioning on the lives of late adolescent girls, aged 18-19. As they stand on the precipice of adulthood, these young women face a world brimming with possibilities and challenges. The transition from adolescence to adulthood is fraught with complex changes—emotional, physical, social, and intellectual. It is a critical period where the seeds of future selves are sown and identities are solidified. This book aims to be a tool for these young women and those who guide them, providing a structured path through the art of questioning to foster growth, understanding, and connectivity.

The Power of Questions

Questions are the simplest yet most profound way of seeking understanding and connection. They can open doors to new knowledge, self-awareness, and deeper relationships. For late adolescent girls, who are navigating the complexities of becoming adults, questions can act as a compass to guide them through uncharted territories. By asking the right questions, we invite introspection and reflection, essential processes for those about to embark on life's vast adventures.

Why Questions Matter

During late adolescence, the significance of building a robust sense of self cannot be overstated. It is a time when young women are making pivotal decisions about their careers, relationships, and beliefs, which will shape their adult lives. Engaging with meaningful questions helps these young women articulate their thoughts, confront their fears, and clarify their aspirations. It empowers them to make choices that align with their values and authentic selves.

Moreover, questions stimulate critical thinking—a skill paramount not only in academic and professional settings but also in personal life where making informed decisions becomes increasingly important. They encourage young women to look beyond obvious answers, fostering a deeper understanding of the world around them and their place within it.

Strengthening Relationships Through Dialogue

Asking and being asked thoughtful questions also enriches relationships. It can transform interactions from superficial exchanges to meaningful dialogues, building trust and empathy among peers, family members, and mentors. For parents and guardians, utilizing these questions can bridge gaps in communication and forge stronger bonds with their adolescent daughters, ensuring a supportive environment where young women feel valued and understood.

The Structure of Our Exploration

This book is structured to mirror the everyday experiences and challenges late-adolescent girls face. Each question has been carefully crafted to encourage deep thought and facilitate personal growth. They cover various topics pertinent to their developmental stage—from self-identity and body image to career aspirations and interpersonal relationships. This approach not only caters to the individual needs of these young women but also supports the adults who play crucial roles in their lives.

A Call to Engage

By the end of this book, the goal is for each reader to have developed a stronger, more nuanced understanding of herself and her relationships. The questions are designed to be revisited, with each answer providing insight that contributes to ongoing personal development. This book is not merely a read; it is an interactive experience, a companion through the transition into adulthood. It aims to inspire confidence, nurture empathy, and foster a resilient spirit, equipping the reader to face the world with curiosity and vigor.

As we embark on this journey together, let us recognize the transformative power of questions. They are not just queries; they are the keys that can unlock the vast potential within each young woman ready to step boldly into the tapestry of adulthood.

Let the journey of questions begin.

Devon & Mauricio

Share Your Experience

Thank you for choosing this book. We hope this has provided meaningful insights and fostered valuable conversations for you and your child.

Your feedback helps us improve and helps other parents and young readers discover this resource. Reviews increase the book's visibility, making it easier for those who might benefit from its content to find it.

If you found this book helpful, please take a moment to leave a review by scanning this QR code.

Your experience can inspire and guide others on their journey of self-discovery and growth. We appreciate your support. Thank you.

Devon & Mauricio

Scan the QR code to access the full collection

Disclaimer

Dear Readers,

This book is designed to serve as a tool for personal growth, reflection, and exploring thoughts and feelings. The questions provided within these pages aim to inspire introspection and conversation, fostering a deeper understanding of oneself and the world.

However, it is important to understand that this book is not a substitute for professional advice, diagnosis, or treatment. While the questions can guide meaningful discussions and self-discovery, they are not intended to address or resolve serious issues or health concerns.

If you or your child encounters significant emotional, psychological, or physical challenges, we strongly recommend seeking the guidance of a qualified professional. This may include consulting a doctor, mental health professional, counselor, or any other relevant specialist who can provide the appropriate support and interventions.

The publisher, author, and any associated parties take no responsibility for any consequences resulting from the use of this book. It is up to the reader to exercise their judgment and discretion when engaging with the questions and interpreting their answers. The insights and reflections gained from this book should be seen as a starting point for further exploration and, when necessary, professional consultation.

We hope that this book serves as a valuable resource for personal growth and development. Remember, each individual's journey of self-discovery is unique, and seeking help when needed is a sign of strength and wisdom.

Guidelines for Asking Questions to Adolescents

Read the following guidelines to learn more about asking questions that unlock learning, foster communication and improve relationships.

- **Effective questions are open or focused, depending on the context**: Questions that open awareness and learning are open-ended questions that cannot be answered with a yes or no. Such questions evoke deeper thinking and reflection.

- **Effective questions support learning**: The goal is to stimulate thinking and deepen understanding of the situation. Insightful questions should focus attention on the most valuable aspects of the issue at hand, helping adolescents understand their experiences and feelings better.

- **Effective questions are asked for the benefit of others**: The intent is to stimulate the thinking and deepen the understanding of adolescents. It is not necessarily about the questioner and their needs.

- **Effective questions engage a personal response**: Engaging adolescents by inviting a personal response—how they feel, what emotions they are bringing to the situation—is crucial. The more a question invites a personal response to a challenge or choice, the more powerful it is for facilitating learning and growth.

- **Effective questions look beyond problems to future outcomes**: When adolescents are entangled in a problem, impactful questions shift the perspective from the problem to the solution, opening new opportunities for action and positive thinking.

- **Effective questions facilitate openness versus defensiveness**: Impactful questions are worded and expressed with a non-judgmental tone and open body language to prevent a defensive reaction. It is usually best to avoid questions that begin with "why" since they often elicit defensive responses or explanations.

- **Effective questions co-create best options versus manipulating outcomes**: Impactful questions are not intended to manipulate or lead adolescents to the option you might think is the best. If you want to suggest, it is best made directly as a suggestion versus a disguised directive through a question.

- **Less is more**: For questions, less is usually more. Ask only one question at a time and avoid long-winded, complicated questions.

Day 1

How do you currently manage your daily nutrition to support your physical and brain development?

Day 2

Can you describe a recent experience that significantly influenced how you see yourself?

Day 3

How do your friendships contribute to your sense of belonging and personal growth?

Day 4

What complex problem have you recently faced, and how did you approach solving it?

Day 5

What is one new skill or knowledge you have acquired this year that you are proud of?

Day 6

What are your main sources of stress, and how do you usually cope with them?

Day 7

How does your cultural background shape your daily life and values?

Day 8

What steps do you take to ensure your physical safety in different environments?

Day 9
Can you think of a time when your moral beliefs were challenged? How did you handle the situation?

Day 10
How often do you spend time in natural settings, and what impact does this have on your mood and health?

Day 11
What forms of physical activity do you enjoy the most, and how often do you participate in them?

Day 12
Describe a situation where you had to manage strong emotions. What strategies helped you?

Day 13

How do you navigate conflicts within your family, and what have you learned from these experiences?

Day 14

In what ways have your literacy and numeracy skills played a crucial role in your everyday life?

Day 15

Reflect on how your ability to communicate has changed over the past few years. What improvements have you noticed?

Day 16

Share an example of a challenge you overcame. What did it teach you about resilience?

Day 17

What influence do you think media has had on your expectations and behaviors?

Day 18

How do you create a secure emotional environment for yourself?

Day 19

How do you explore and nurture your spiritual beliefs and values?

Day 20

What are the most significant differences you've observed between urban and rural lifestyles, and how do they impact you?

Day 21
How have the physical changes during puberty affected your self-image and confidence?

Day 22
Can you share an instance where understanding someone else's feelings changed your perspective?

Day 23
How do you manage your self-presentation and relationships online?

Day 24
What learning style works best for you, and how do you utilize it to enhance your education?

Day 25

What social skills do you feel you have mastered, and which do you think you need to develop further?

Day 26

Why do you think awareness and treatment of mental health issues are important in your community?

Day 27

How has your socioeconomic background influenced the opportunities and challenges you face?

Day 28

What measures do you take to protect yourself from online risks like cyberbullying and privacy breaches?

Day 29
Describe a situation where you had to make a tough ethical decision. What factors did you consider?

Day 30
How do you think individual actions contribute to environmental preservation?

Day 31
How do you balance rest and physical activity, and why is this balance important to you?

Day 32
What personal achievement are you most proud of, and what does it say about your values and priorities?

Day 33

How do you handle disagreements with friends, and what do you think it teaches you about relationships?

Day 34

What goals have you set for the next five years, and how do you plan to achieve them?

Day 35

How has your understanding of your own emotions helped you in your personal relationships?

Day 36

In what ways do you seek out emotional support when you're feeling overwhelmed?

Day 37
How has social media influenced your views on body image and self-worth?

Day 38
What are your strategies for dealing with peer pressure, especially in uncomfortable situations?

Day 39
Discuss a time when you felt a strong connection to your cultural heritage. What sparked this feeling?

Day 40
How do you ensure your online interactions are positive and safe?

Day 41

When faced with a moral dilemma, who do you turn to for advice, and why?

Day 42

How do you approach learning new information that challenges your existing beliefs or knowledge?

Day 43

What part of your daily routine is most important for maintaining your mental health, and why?

Day 44

How do you prioritize tasks and manage time when you feel overwhelmed by responsibilities?

Day 45
Describe a moment when you felt very connected to nature. What was the situation, and how did it make you feel?

Day 46
What book or movie had a significant impact on your understanding of the world, and why?

Day 47
How do you navigate maintaining your privacy and security in digital spaces?

Day 48
What are some of the most significant pressures you feel from society, and how do you handle them?

Day 49

How do you deal with feelings of anxiety or stress before a significant event or exam?

Day 50

What role does physical exercise play in your life, and how does it affect your mood and energy levels?

Day 51

Describe a relationship that has taught you something valuable about yourself.

Day 52

How do you celebrate your achievements, and why do you think it's important to do so?

Day 53
What are the key factors you consider when making decisions about your future?

Day 54
How has a failure or setback shaped your outlook and approach to new challenges?

Day 55
What strategies do you use to enhance your learning and retention when studying new subjects?

Day 56
How do you balance your personal life and academic or career obligations?

Day 57
What has been your most effective method for building new friendships and maintaining old ones?

Day 58
How do you approach conversations about difficult topics with people who have different views from yours?

Day 59
What are the essential components of a healthy and supportive relationship?

Day 60
How do you practice self-care, and why do you think it's important?

Day 61
What recent changes have you noticed about your physical health, and what do you attribute these changes to?

Day 62
Discuss an experience where you had to lead a group. What did you learn about leadership and teamwork?

Day 63
How do you deal with the challenge of balancing screen time and personal interactions?

Day 64
In what ways do you contribute to your community, and what motivates you to do so?

Day 65
How do you handle criticism, and what steps do you take to use it constructively?

Day 66
What traditions are important in your family, and how do they influence your sense of identity?

Day 67
When have you felt most empowered, and what were the circumstances?

Day 68
What creative outlets do you pursue, and how do they enhance your well-being?

Day 69
How do you determine what information is credible when you encounter conflicting sources online?

Day 70
What are your strategies for managing long-term projects or assignments effectively?

Day 71
How do you approach setting boundaries in personal and professional relationships?

Day 72
What are your thoughts on the importance of community service and volunteer work?

Day 73

How do you approach maintaining a balance between tradition and modernity in your life?

Day 74

What are your views on the importance of mental health education in schools?

Day 75

How do you manage your expectations when embarking on new relationships or friendships?

Day 76

What measures do you take to stay informed about current events and their implications?

Day 77

How do you stay motivated when faced with repetitive or monotonous tasks?

Day 78

Discuss a time when you had to adapt to a significant change. What strategies helped you cope?

Day 79

What is your approach to managing financial responsibilities?

Day 80

How do you evaluate and decide on your involvement in extracurricular activities or hobbies?

Day 81
What steps do you take to foster a positive self-image and combat negative thoughts?

Day 82
What role do mentors or role models play in your life, and how do you choose them?

Day 83
How do you address and manage the expectations set by your parents or guardians?

Day 84
In what ways have your experiences shaped your views on independence and autonomy?

Day 85

How do you approach conflict resolution in a way that respects both parties' viewpoints?

Day 86

What are your strategies for staying focused and productive when you're not motivated?

Day 87

How do you maintain a balance between your personal privacy and your desire to share on social media?

Day 88

What kind of support system do you have, and how has it helped you during tough times?

Day 89
How do you decide which college or career path is right for you?

Day 90
What has been the most challenging aspect of transitioning into adulthood?

Day 91
How do you prepare for important decisions, and what resources do you use to inform those decisions?

Day 92
What is your approach to building and maintaining trust in a relationship?

Day 93
How do you define success, and how has your definition evolved over time?

Day 94
What experiences have taught you the most about yourself?

Day 95
How do you handle the pressure to conform to social norms and expectations?

Day 96
What are some ways you've learned to cope with rejection or disappointment?

Day 97

How do you prioritize your mental and physical health during busy times?

Day 98

What strategies do you employ to manage stress during exams or major projects?

Day 99

How do you cultivate a sense of purpose and direction in your life?

Day 100

What measures do you take to foster healthy communication in your relationships?

Day 101
How do you deal with change, especially when unexpected or unwanted?

Day 102
What actions do you take to strengthen your resilience against adversity?

Day 103
How has your understanding of friendship evolved as you have grown older?

Day 104
What steps do you take to ensure that you are treated with respect by peers and adults?

Day 105
How do you determine the most important values to you, and how do you uphold them?

Day 106
What are the most effective ways you have found to manage your time efficiently?

Day 107
How do you handle feelings of isolation or loneliness?

Day 108
What activities help you reconnect with yourself when you feel out of touch?

Day 109
How do you approach learning and personal growth outside of formal education?

Day 110
What has been your biggest learning experience from travelling or interacting with different cultures?

Day 111
How do you manage the balance between saving and spending?

Day 112
What are your strategies for overcoming fears or anxieties that hold you back?

Day 113
How do you build confidence in areas where you feel insecure?

Day 114
What role does creativity play in your personal and academic life?

Day 115
How do you stay informed and critical in a world with so much information?

Day 116
What has been your approach to finding meaningful friendships and connections?

Day 117
How do you handle the expectations to achieve certain life milestones by specific ages?

Day 118
What are some of the ways you contribute to promoting a sustainable and healthy environment?

Day 119
How do you navigate the complexities of modern relationships?

Day 120
What are your methods for keeping track of personal goals and assessing your progress?

Day 121
How do you respond to and recover from personal setbacks?

Day 122
What techniques do you use to enhance your problem-solving skills?

Day 123
How do you handle peer comparisons, especially on platforms like social media?

Day 124
What has been a significant moment of self-discovery for you?

Day 125
How do you ensure that you are listening and responding effectively in conversations?

Day 126
What steps do you take to challenge yourself and step out of your comfort zone?

Day 127
How do you navigate the challenges of maintaining a healthy lifestyle?

Day 128
What impact has volunteering or community service had on your perspective and personal growth?

Day 129
What have you learned about yourself from romantic relationships?

Day 130
How do you approach making amends after a disagreement or conflict?

Day 131
What steps do you take to stay motivated and engaged in your studies or work?

Day 132
What personal values guide your decisions and how did you come to hold them?

Day 133
How do you approach balancing your own needs with the expectations of others?

Day 134
What strategies do you use to maintain a positive outlook during difficult times?

Day 135
What role has your education played in shaping your worldview?

Day 136
How do you assess the reliability of news and information you receive?

Day 137
What are the most significant challenges you foresee in your transition to adulthood?

Day 138
How do you manage distractions to maintain focus on your goals?

Day 139
What are your thoughts on lifelong learning and self-improvement?

Day 140
How do you define a healthy relationship, and what are its key components?

Day 141
What have you learned from a recent mistake, and how has it influenced your actions?

Day 142
How do you manage the balance between work or school and your personal life?

Day 143
What are your main criteria for choosing friends, and how have these choices impacted your life?

Day 144
What are the essential elements of trust for you in a relationship?

Day 145
How do you stay resilient despite societal pressures on appearance and behavior?

Day 146
What are some of the ways you show kindness to others?

Day 147
How do you handle the stress of uncertainty about the future?

Day 148
What are the most important factors you consider when planning for your career?

Day 149
How do you approach taking risks and stepping out of your comfort zone?

Day 150
What personal achievements are you aiming for in the next year?

Day 151
How do you prioritize your tasks and commitments to manage your time effectively?

Day 152
What strategies do you find most effective for learning new skills or subjects?

Day 153
How do you cope with feelings of inadequacy or self-doubt?

Day 154
What steps do you take to maintain your physical health aside from exercise?

Day 155
How do you stay connected with your cultural roots and traditions?

Day 156
What motivates you to keep going even when you face significant challenges?

Day 157
How do you ensure that your personal values align with your actions?

Day 158
What have you learned about love and relationships from your family?

Day 159
How do you approach conflicts in a way that leads to growth and resolution?

Day 160
What are your strategies for constructively dealing with negative emotions?

Day 161
How do you build and maintain personal discipline in various aspects of your life?

Day 162
What are your thoughts on the impact of technology on personal relationships?

Day 163
How do you ensure fairness in your interactions with others?

Day 164
What lessons have you learned about managing money effectively?

Day 165
How do you deal with the fear of failure?

Day 166
What has been your experience with leadership, and what have you learned from it?

Day 167
How do you approach ethical dilemmas in your daily life?

Day 168
What are the qualities you look for in a mentor or leader?

Day 169
How do you ensure that you are continuously growing and developing personally?

Day 170
What are your thoughts on the importance of having a routine?

Day 171
How do you stay grounded in the face of success or praise?

Day 172
What are your techniques for effective communication in challenging situations?

Day 173
How do you deal with the pressure to succeed academically or professionally?

Day 174
What are the most significant barriers you've faced in achieving your goals, and how have you overcome them?

Day 175
How do you balance individuality and conformity in your social circles?

Day 176
What steps do you take to cultivate empathy and understanding in your relationships?

Day 177
How do you approach decision-making when faced with multiple good options?

Day 178
What role do hobbies and leisure activities play in your life?

Day 179
What has been your approach to dealing with loss or grief?

Day 180
What practices help you stay mindful and present in your daily life?

Day 181
How do you approach maintaining mental wellness alongside physical fitness?

Day 182
How do you handle expectations from your family regarding your career or educational choices?

Day 183
What strategies do you find most helpful in relieving stress during demanding times?

Day 184
How do you approach setting and pursuing personal goals that are important to you?

Day 185
In what ways do you contribute to creating a supportive and inclusive environment among your peers?

Day 186
How do you handle social situations where you feel out of place or uncomfortable?

Day 187
What has been your most significant learning from a cultural exchange or interaction with someone from a different background?

Day 188
How do you deal with procrastination when it impacts your goals?

Day 189
What measures do you take to protect your mental health in a hyper-connected world?

Day 190
How do you define personal success, and what steps are you taking to achieve it?

Day 191
What are your strategies for maintaining a work-life balance, especially when both demand your attention?

Day 192
How do you deal with the challenges of adapting to changes in technology as it evolves?

Day 193
What role does gratitude play in your life, and how do you practice it?

Day 194
How do you determine the authenticity of relationships in your life?

Day 195
What actions do you take to ensure your actions reflect your ethical beliefs?

Day 196
How do you prioritize self-improvement and personal development activities?

Day 197
What techniques do you use to stay calm in high-pressure situations?

Day 198
How do you handle feelings of envy or jealousy towards others?

Day 199
What are your methods for building a strong and supportive community around you?

Day 200
How do you maintain your identity and values in a society that may have different expectations?

Day 201
How do you approach learning from experiences that are outside of your comfort zone?

Day 202
What has been your experience with maintaining friendships as you and your friends grow and change?

Day 203
How do you handle situations where you have to lead others who may be older or more experienced than you?

Day 204
What steps do you take to foster creativity in your everyday life?

Day 205
How do you navigate making decisions that affect both your personal and professional life?

Day 206
What has been the most helpful feedback you've received, and how did it help you grow?

Day 207
How do you manage the balance between giving and receiving in relationships?

Day 208
What steps do you take to stay engaged and motivated in tasks you find less interesting?

Day 209
How do you handle transitions, such as moving from school to university or entering the workforce?

Day 210
What has been a key factor in developing your self-awareness?

Day 211
How do you approach conflict resolution with someone who has a different perspective?

Day 212
What role does physical health play in your overall well-being and productivity?

Day 213

How do you approach the challenge of balancing personal desires with professional obligations?

Day 214

What methods do you use to evaluate your personal growth and development over time?

Day 215

How do you manage the pressures of social expectations regarding marriage, career, or lifestyle?

Day 216

What practices do you find most effective for nurturing your mental and emotional health?

Day 217
How do you deal with the challenge of maintaining friendships in a busy world?

Day 218
What experiences have significantly shaped your outlook on life?

Day 219
How do you prioritize which relationships to nurture and devote time to?

Day 220
What are the most effective ways you've found to manage financial stress?

Day 221
How do you deal with uncertainty and unpredictability in your life?

Day 222
What has been your strategy for developing effective communication skills?

Day 223
How do you maintain a sense of community and belonging, especially in new or changing environments?

Day 224
What steps do you take to develop and maintain patience in your personal and professional life?

Day 225
How do you balance accepting yourself as you are while also striving for self-improvement?

Day 226
What strategies do you use to enhance your decision-making skills?

Day 227
How do you handle the pressure to perform well in competitive environments?

Day 228
What practices do you follow to ensure you stay true to your personal and professional goals?

Day 229

What measures do you take to manage and mitigate the impact of stress on your health?

Day 230

How do you approach dealing with criticism and feedback in a constructive way?

Day 231

What techniques do you employ to maintain focus and discipline in your academic or professional pursuits?

Day 232

How do you evaluate when to push your boundaries and when to honor your limits?

Day 233
In what ways do you seek to understand viewpoints different from your own?

Day 234
How do you handle the tension between pursuing personal passions and practical responsibilities?

Day 235
What steps do you take to ensure you're not overwhelmed by the opinions of others on social media?

Day 236
How do you maintain a sense of self in relationships without losing your independence?

Day 237
What actions do you take to cultivate a healthy self-esteem?

Day 238
How do you deal with the fear of the unknown in major life decisions?

Day 239
What role do hobbies play in your personal and emotional development?

Day 240
How do you manage the challenge of keeping personal and professional life separate?

Day 241
How do you approach maintaining a positive attitude when faced with setbacks?

Day 242
What steps do you take to ensure that you are making ethical choices in your everyday life?

Day 243
How do you handle the balance of taking care of yourself while supporting others?

Day 244
What are the most important lessons you have learned from your relationships?

Day 245
How do you manage the pressure to make decisions about your future?

Day 246
What strategies do you employ to recover from emotional exhaustion?

Day 247
How do you ensure that your goals align with your core values?

Day 248
What has been your experience with balancing personal desires with family expectations?

Day 249
How do you approach maintaining friendships as your life paths diverge?

Day 250
What methods do you use to stay grounded when experiencing rapid changes in your life?

Day 251
How do you manage and allocate your time effectively between work, study, and leisure?

Day 252
What are some key strategies you use to enhance your interpersonal skills?

Day 253
How do you approach setting boundaries to maintain a healthy lifestyle?

Day 254
What actions do you take to remain focused and motivated towards long-term goals?

Day 255
How do you approach integrating new habits into your daily routine?

Day 256
What measures do you take to build resilience in the face of adversity?

Day 257
How do you assess the impact of your actions on others?

Day 258
What strategies do you find effective for dealing with distractions in your daily life?

Day 259
How do you handle the challenge of staying informed without becoming overwhelmed by information?

Day 260
What are your approaches to resolving conflicts without compromising your values?

Day 261
How do you ensure that you are proactive in your personal and professional development?

Day 262
What methods do you employ to manage stress in a healthy way?

Day 263
How do you handle competing priorities in your personal and professional life?

Day 264
What practices do you follow to enhance your creative thinking and problem-solving skills?

Day 265
How do you manage the challenge of adapting to new environments or cultures?

Day 266
What strategies do you use to keep your emotional well-being in check while navigating social pressures?

Day 267
How do you approach the process of self-reflection and self-improvement?

Day 268
What steps do you take to develop a supportive network of friends and colleagues?

Day 269
How do you deal with setbacks in achieving your personal goals?

Day 270
What methods do you use to maintain a balanced approach to life's demands?

Day 271
How do you cultivate a culture of learning and growth within your social or professional circles?

Day 272
What steps do you take to maintain honesty and integrity in your actions?

Day 273
How do you handle situations where you must stand up for your beliefs in the face of opposition?

Day 274
What are your strategies for maintaining enthusiasm and energy in your daily activities?

Day 275
How do you approach the challenge of building and maintaining trust in new relationships?

Day 276
What practices do you adopt to manage your time and energy effectively?

Day 277
How do you navigate personal growth while maintaining important relationships?

Day 278
What techniques do you find most effective in managing your emotional responses to stressful situations?

Day 279
How do you decide which aspects of your life need more attention or improvement?

Day 280
What strategies do you use to stay engaged and active in your community?

Day 281
How do you balance your personal convictions with the need to be flexible in your thinking?

Day 282
What has been the most challenging aspect of managing your personal finances?

Day 283
How do you foster a positive environment that encourages mutual respect and understanding among your peers?

Day 284
What steps do you take to avoid burnout in both your personal and professional life?

Day 285
How do you deal with the pressure to excel in every area of your life?

Day 286
What methods do you use to stay organized and keep track of various commitments and responsibilities?

Day 287
How do you handle the integration of new members into your social or work circles?

Day 288
What practices do you employ to ensure that you remain honest and transparent in your communications?

Day 289
How do you maintain your individuality while also adapting to group norms and expectations?

Day 290
What have been some key factors in maintaining enduring friendships?

Day 291
How do you determine when to seek help or advice from others?

Day 292
What methods have you found effective in overcoming fears about the future?

Day 293
How do you balance the need for personal space with the desire to be socially active?

Day 294
What steps do you take to maintain and cultivate new interests and hobbies?

Day 295
How do you manage the impact of social media on your self-esteem and personal relationships?

Day 296
What strategies have you developed to handle the emotional challenges of adult relationships?

Day 297
How do you evaluate success in your personal development and achievements?

Day 298
What role does reflection play in your personal growth, and how often do you engage in it?

Day 299
How do you cope with the challenges of sudden life changes or unexpected events?

Day 300
What has been your approach to maintaining a healthy work-life balance during transitional phases of life?

Day 301

How do you manage the tension between following your passion and securing a stable career?

Day 302

What strategies do you employ to keep yourself motivated when progress seems slow or negligible?

Day 303

How do you address the challenge of making long-term commitments, whether personal or professional?

Day 304

What practices have you found helpful in maintaining mental clarity and focus during stressful times?

Day 305
How do you deal with comparisons, whether with peers in your age group or different generations?

Day 306
What actions do you take to ensure you're growing in your career or academic pursuits?

Day 307
How do you manage relationships with people who have significantly different life experiences or values?

Day 308
What are some ways you've found effective for expressing gratitude in your daily life?

Day 309
How do you navigate the balance between giving and receiving advice?

Day 310
What strategies do you use to reconcile personal goals with external expectations?

Day 311
How do you deal with the challenge of staying true to yourself in highly competitive environments?

Day 312
What steps do you take to ensure that your physical health supports your mental and emotional well-being?

Day 313
How do you approach the process of forgiving others and moving forward from conflict?

Day 314
What are the most effective ways you have found to advocate for your needs and desires?

Day 315
How do you handle moments of self-doubt and uncertainty about your future?

Day 316
What techniques have you employed to enhance your leadership skills?

Day 317
How do you ensure that your personal and professional lives enhance, rather than detract from, each other?

Day 318
What steps have you taken to understand and improve your emotional intelligence?

Day 319
How do you approach maintaining a balance between learning and doing in your personal and professional development?

Day 320
What are some effective ways you have found to manage your time when juggling multiple responsibilities?

Day 321
How do you discern which relationships are worth investing more energy into?

Day 322
What strategies do you employ to manage and overcome personal insecurities?

Day 323
How do you maintain a healthy lifestyle amidst the demands of school or work?

Day 324
What practices help you to stay calm and composed under pressure?

Day 325
How do you approach the challenge of maintaining a positive self-image?

Day 326
What has been your experience with setting and maintaining boundaries in your relationships?

Day 327
How do you determine the best approach to learning something new, whether a skill or concept?

Day 328
What methods have you found effective for dealing with disappointment or setbacks?

Day 329
How do you ensure that your actions reflect your long-term goals?

Day 330
What key factors do you consider when forming an opinion on a contentious issue?

Day 331
How do you handle the dynamics of group work or collaborative projects?

Day 332
What steps do you take to listen and ensure others feel heard actively?

Day 333
How do you deal with the pressures of making important life choices?

Day 334
What role does self-reflection play in your approach to personal growth?

Day 335
How do you maintain enthusiasm for your pursuits when faced with routine or monotony?

Day 336
What has been a crucial factor in developing and sustaining your work ethic?

Day 337
How do you navigate the challenges of changing social circles or friendships?

Day 338
What practices do you find most helpful in maintaining mental health stability?

Day 339
How do you assess the impact of your lifestyle choices on your overall well-being?

Day 340
What has been your approach to dealing with cultural or societal norms that you disagree with?

Day 341
How do you balance your need for security with the desire for freedom and adventure?

Day 342
What strategies have you developed to deal with peer pressure effectively?

Day 343
How do you ensure that your personal values guide your daily actions and decisions?

Day 344
What steps have you taken to cultivate a supportive and encouraging network?

Day 345
How do you approach handling feedback, both positive and negative?

Day 346
What methods do you use to stay informed and make educated decisions?

Day 347
How do you manage the impact of external expectations on your self-esteem and personal goals?

Day 348
What has been your experience with personal growth through volunteer or charity work?

Day 349
How do you ensure that you are not unduly influenced by the opinions of others?

Day 350
What practices do you implement to remain adaptable in the face of change?

Day 351
How do you balance the pursuit of your passions with the responsibilities of adult life?

Day 352
What has been the most effective way for you to handle conflicts within your family?

Day 353
How do you stay motivated during periods of low activity or downtime?

Day 354
What steps do you take to ensure your physical activities positively affect your mental health?

Day 355
How do you navigate the complexity of maintaining a personal identity in a digital world?

Day 356
How do you ensure your career choices align with your life goals?

Day 357
How do you handle the stress related to uncertainty about your future career or educational path?

Day 358
What has been a key lesson you've learned from a significant challenge or obstacle?

Day 359
How do you ensure that your personal ambitions do not overshadow your relationships?

Day 360
What practices have you adopted to manage stress without compromising your personal or professional integrity?

Day 361
How do you cultivate and maintain a sense of curiosity and wonder?

Day 362
What steps do you take to remain proactive about your health and wellness?

Day 363
How do you determine when to step back and take a break from your responsibilities?

Day 364
What methods have you found effective in reconciling personal aspirations with societal expectations?

Day 365
How do you celebrate your personal achievements and milestones?

Share Your Experience

Thank you for choosing this book. We hope this has provided meaningful insights and fostered valuable conversations for you and your child.

Your feedback helps us improve and helps other parents and young readers discover this resource. Reviews increase the book's visibility, making it easier for those who might benefit from its content to find it.

If you found this book helpful, please take a moment to leave a review by scanning this QR code.

Your experience can inspire and guide others on their journey of self-discovery and growth. We appreciate your support. Thank you.

Devon & Mauricio

www.ingramcontent.com/pod-product-compliance
Lightning Source LLC
Chambersburg PA
CBHW081337120626
46546CB00011B/3392